THE ORIGIN OF MY FAITH

Other Books by the Author

A Rose Will Grow Anywhere
Amazed By Grace: The Miracle of God's Love
Before You Call, I Will Answer
Flagler & His Church
Getting Through the Night
God is Up To Something
He Never Spoke without a Parable Vol. 1: Your Neighbor
He Never Spoke without a Parable Vol. 2: Your Father
He Never Spoke without a Parable Vol. 3: His Kingdom
He Never Spoke without a Parable Vol. 4: Your Antagonist
He Never Spoke without a Parable Vol. 5: It's Up to You
If I Could Pray Again
Jesus Makes Me Laugh, republished as *Jesus Makes Me Laugh with Him;* also published in Portuguese.
Lives He Touched: The Relationships of Jesus
Never Lose Heart
Songs in the Night
The Couch and the Altar
The Faith of Our Fathers
The Golden String
The Miracles and the Parables: Two Best Sellers Complete in One Volume
The Miracles of Christ
The New Immorality
The Parables He Told
The Prayers I Love (two publishers, one Celestial Arts)
The Psalms of David
Until You Bless Me
What is the Man?

You may find his available books for sale on his website, www.davidredding.com
secured by PayPal.

The Origin of My Faith

DAVID A. REDDING

Laity Lodge
H. E. Butt Foundation
P. O. Box 290670, Kerrville, Texas 78029-0670
Phone: 830-896-2505

Book Design: The DesignWorks Group

ISBN: 978-0-9671701-7-6

Copyright David A. Redding, 2009
Cover painting by Dorothy McCleery Redding of an image of David's boyhood home near Kilgore, Ohio.

*To my wife, cousin, and best friend,
who died on the eve of my final year
at this source of the river
sacred to us as to the Celts.*

*Dorothy Ruth McCleery Redding
May 14, 1927 - April 7, 2008*

Acknowledgements

There is no way I can cover my indebtedness to Howard E. Butt, Jr., Founder of Laity Lodge, as well as my lifelong friend and counselor, his wife, Barbara Dan, and to his son-in-law, David Rogers, and his wife, Deborah Butt Rogers. The chief officers of this unique Eden in the Hill Country of Texas have not only been my colleagues, but my bosom friends: Dwight Lacy, Bill Cody, Howard Hovde, Eddie Sears, David Williamson, and many others.

How much I owe this miniature Grand Canyon, the work of nature it is that works its wonders on everyone who comes! These are the last addresses I delivered during the series of Creativity Weeks that began in the early 1970s and ended in June 2008. They are dedicated to those who heard and survived them.

Cyra Dimitru, Visiting Lecturer in English Literature and Writing, St. Mary's University in San Antonio, has been an excellent editor and proofreader, and Keith Mirrer, Director of Communications, Foundations for Laity Renewal, won my warmest appreciation.

Gratitude also goes to my daughter, Marion T. Redding, who has been my indispensible assistant.

The Author
Sky Farm, Ohio

Table of Contents

THE ORIGIN OF MY FAITH: THE SHEPHERD BOY	1
THE FAITH OF MY CHILDREN	7
MY FATHER'S FAITH: LITTLE BROTHER	13
IN HARM'S WAY: MY WORLD WAR II	19
THE SOURCE OF THE RIVER IS SACRED	27
YOU TAUGHT ME HOW TO DANCE	35
TABLE OF FIGURES	36
A WORD ABOUT THE ARTIST: DAVID M. REDDING	37
ABOUT THE AUTHOR: DAVID A. REDDING	38

Figure 1: "Five Smooth Stones: The Shepherd Boy," by David M. Redding

The Origin of My Faith: The Shepherd Boy

DAVID'S TWENTY-THIRD PSALM

> The LORD is my shepherd; I shall not want.
> He maketh me to lie down in green pastures:
> he leadeth me beside the still waters.
> He restoreth my soul:
> he leadeth me in the paths of righteousness for his name's sake.
> Yea, though I walk through the valley of the shadow of death,
> I will fear no evil: for thou art with me;
> thy rod and thy staff they comfort me.
> Thou preparest a table before me in the presence of mine enemies:
> thou anointest my head with oil; my cup runneth over.
> Surely goodness and mercy shall follow me all the days of my life:
> and I will dwell in the house of the LORD for ever.
>
> (PSALM 23)

Early mornings my Scottish mother kept her tears of sorrow and despair where they fell on the pages of the prayers that are the Psalms. She would pour over the Psalms faithfully as the growing light of dawn cast its shadows. As a child, I caught hints of the help she received from the time spent with the Psalms, hints that grew with me over time.

Knowing her, I had no trouble understanding why the famous Jewish Soviet Dissident prisoner, Natan Sharansky, sat down and refused to march further despite beatings, until the guards returned his well-thumbed copy of the Psalms.

Jesus quoted from the Psalms more than any other book. It was the only book he quoted from the Cross.

It is no wonder that St. Gennadius, the Patriarch of Constantinople, would not ordain anyone who could not recite the Psalter. Sir Thomas More, England's scholarly Lord Chancellor, bravely stood up to the dreaded Henry VIII, and faced the ax of his executioner with words like wings from Psalm 51. Benjamin Franklin broke the deadlock of our Constitutional Convention with words of Psalm 127.

There was a time when our fathers learned as children at their mothers' knees the words of the Bible, and particularly those of the Psalms. They kept those words by heart, until they found them on their lips as they left this life. Today the Bible is nearly forgotten. The lordly language of this magnificent tradition in the western world has fallen beneath our feet. Our busy hands can't be still and don't have time for holding the pages of the Bible open. The Ten Commandments are no longer at our command, commanding us.

Until recently, hardly a funeral could take place in our country even for someone who had never seen the inside of a church, without the twenty-third Psalm's beloved benediction. It has been cherished for over three thousand years, although it came to us from the other side of the world. It has no name and is known only by a number: the twenty-third Psalm. The fragment of Scripture that might still come to the mind of someone who is dying can be found indexed by its first line, "The Lord is my shepherd."

Once there was a lad alone in a desolate wilderness on the eastern shore of the Mediterranean named David. Imagine a typical boy exiled to brush-covered rocky hills with no other boy to talk to, no father to go to, starved for his mother's cooking, afraid that the other boys were getting the pick of the girls, and afraid that even the servants were stealing his old father's prize parcels of the inheritance. Imagine the nightmares that the wilderness and the days without end must have caused him. Yet, instead of going insane as many do who are abandoned, David finds himself. He also finds the God that is "nearer than hands or feet."

This unusual young psalmist discovers that he has not been deserted; his isolation is the best thing to happen to him. For with every other distraction out of the way, God comes into focus and in full color. These remote hills yield powerful secrets to him. Magellan and Einstein were not to be our only explorers. David becomes our explorer of the spiritual world.

We cannot accuse David of being naïve. Disasters preferred his time. His own people had stacks of sacked cities in their repertoire. It was customary then for the enemy to rape and massacre the women and children of vanquished cities. David also knew all too well about wolves getting into the sheep, and sheep getting lost.

Yet, in the midst of it all, this unbelievable youth can't wait to tune his strings. All alone in the wilderness he sings his way out. And, he sets the stage for his divine descendant, Jesus, to announce that one lost sheep was worth leaving ninety-nine. "Ninety-nine are not enough for God."

David was one hero who was not so carried away by his triumph over a lion and a bear to miss what invisible hands had done for him. He knows he does not have the eye of a falcon nor the strength of an ox; he did not whip the lion and the bear alone. He senses that someone stood him on his feet and steadied his sling. Without that crucial assistance, he would have been as good as dead, like any sheep being shorn. His flock has taught him about being vulnerable. They are doomed, just as he found he is, without their shepherd.

The introductory line of Psalm 23 celebrates David's discovery. "The Lord is my shepherd." Kings identify themselves with eagles and lions. Instead of a flattering royal portrait, this ruthlessly honest boy sees himself as a sheep; he admits he is as dumb and helpless as any old ewe. He admits that he is powerless as a single ram trying to defeat a pack of wolves. He declares that not only has God shepherded his flock from being devoured by a lion and a bear, God has also saved him and his nation from a sword as huge as a weaver's beam and wielded by a giant named Goliath. Then David goes even further. He has the humility to realize that he is not God's pet; he is not deserving of any special favors. No wonder that the Savior of the world becomes identified not as the son of Abraham (God's friend), nor as the son of Moses (God's lawyer), but rather as "the Son of David."[1]

"I shall not want." David's perspective affords him fresh appreciation of each fig he picks and hare he traps. For a sheep there is no relief, no protection, no good grass without the shepherd.

"Yea, though I walk through the valley of the shadow of death, I will fear no evil for Thou art with me." Legends from ancient Palestine refer to a death-defying gorge through which sheep had to be led to the succulent summer forage of the high country. Yet, death not only lurked in the gorge, its fatal jaws waited anywhere

---

[1] The first name given to the Psalms was "Prayers" or "Tehilloth." The word "praises" or "Psalms" was coined from their musical accompaniment. While the book seems to have been written by several hands, it is not without reason that it bears the name of David, "Psalms of David." Surely David with his heart of gold was the shepherd who composed this gem.

off of the main trail. Sheep easily lose their way; they don't have a homing instinct as do cats and dogs or even birds. A lost sheep has to wait until it is found. Death doesn't always cast a long shadow. That ultimate surprise might spring upon us around the next corner. What can compare to having a bodyguard whose rod and staff are equal to the jaws of death: life's wolf itself?

As David continues with, "Thou preparest a table before me in the presence of my enemies" he does not suggest a condemned man's last meal on death row. Jesus, in the presence of Judas, picks up David's celebration, with his own Last Supper. What other reason than the joyful wedding of heaven and earth could David and Jesus possibly have for setting the table at such a dreadful time? Who would feel like eating then?

"Thou anointed my head with oil." Oil was the major medicine to protect sheep from the plague of insects and sores. The Good Samaritan "poured on oil and wine" to heal the lacerations of the half-dead victim "who fell among the thieves." Oil was used to bless and confess dying people, preparing them for God. Kings were anointed with oil as they were consecrated.

"My cup runneth over." The expensive restaurant today pours our glass half full. But any host worthy of the name in the Middle East pours his guest's cup until it is spilling. This is the generosity of the Lord God who spangled His sky with stars, and who worked the first miracle of the Lord Jesus when He changed a great quantity of water into expensive wine at a poor man's wedding.

"Surely goodness and mercy will follow me all the days of my life, and I shall dwell in the house of the Lord." As long as I live? Where is that house? No one would last in an empty church. God's holy place is not here. Surely the psalmist does not mean only an overnight stay. God wouldn't be much of a shepherd with only a temporary appointment. Some scholars insist upon replacing the last word "forever" (used by the King James translation) with the words "As long as I live." However, the bountiful care ultimately fulfilled by the Good Shepherd Himself strongly suggests that the psalmist anticipated the infinite hospitality that would eventually be offered through Jesus Christ. Psalm 23 itself calls for the words that spill: forever.

Figure 2: "The Accident," by David M. Redding

The Faith of My Children

All praise to Thee, my God this night, for all the blessings of the light;
Keep me, O keep me, King of Kings, beneath the shadow of Thy wings.

(TALLIS' CANON, THOMAS KEN, BASED ON PSALMS 42:8 AND 17:8)

    Summers we always spent time in a cabin we built in the woods. We picked what we called "The Cabin Song." It was from the Psalms, printed above. When our youngest son was two and a half he had to have a hernia operation. As he left us, on the gurney for that first journey into the darkness alone, he started singing that song, that echoed as they wheeled him down the hallway. We could still hear him as the elevator doors closed.

My youngest son took hold of his life, and immediately gave it to God.

At three he made his first move. He had finally made enough trips to the women's bathroom. His golden opportunity to be himself took place on the interstate as we traveled on vacation. His mother led him to their usual door.

"Mom, what does it say up there?"

"Women."

He let go of her hand and identified himself, "I'm not supposed to go in there!"

Dee rolled her eyes and handed him over to me. When we reached the threshold of "my place," he repeated his question. "Dad, what does it say up there?"

"Men."

He walked in unassisted. And, in a strong voice he made the official announcement of his coveted entrance into the fraternity of colleagues lined up against the wall, "Hi, Men!"

It was not long until he made his next move to further demonstrate his identity. He and his brothers grew up in the 1960s when it was almost compulsory for boys to go around unshorn like Visigoths. As a former Navy Deck Officer in the Pacific during World War II, I detested the style. As a father, I ignored the crime that was taking place under my own nose in my own family until I had the honor of handing out diplomas to the kindergartners. I hardly recognized the last graduate beneath his luxuriant foliage. As he extended his hand to receive his diploma, I couldn't resist inquiring, "Son, who cuts your hair?"

He shoved up his forelock and replied, "Aw, Dad, you know it's Mom."

That night I said to Dee, "Our son looks like a hedgehog."

"He wants to look like his older brothers. They're doing fine in school, aren't they?"

"Yes."

"Have they been skipping church?"

"No."

"Then why can't our sons decide how they cut their hair?"

"Well."

"Why not let God work it out with them?"

When my son turned eleven, we traveled as a family to Florence, Italy – thanks to the generosity of Dee's father. By then, my son's hair fell below his shoulders. Less than a week into the trip, my son confronted his mother. "Mom, I want you to cut my hair. Short. Now. Please."

"Why?"

"Soon as the guys get off their motorcycles, they crowd around to pinch me." Dee fulfilled our son's request. I was reminded again of her wisdom as a mother.

My son grew into a six-foot-four-inch giant; we still called him "Little Irrepressible." Not everyone found him endearing. He and one of his junior high teachers did not get along. In fact, she predicted, "There's one boy who will end up behind bars." Although we managed to avoid motorcycles with his older brothers, my son did earn the largest trail bike I have ever seen when he was fifteen. He and I promised Dee that it would only be ridden on the farm. He kept that promise; I did not.

The day that we moved up the hill to the new stone house we had built, I asked my son to run an errand on his bike. It meant driving along the forbidden state route. He had no license. Excited by this adventure, he turned from our lane and gunned the bike onto the highway. I heard the screech of tires, a crash, and what sounded like the cracking of a sapling. I raced to him. He was lying beside the road still astride the motorcycle. His leg, which I had heard break, was nearly torn off.

Several internists recommended that we amputate the leg immediately, and not risk gangrene. Our beloved family physician Dr. Herman Karrer told us, "I know of only one surgeon who would try to save that leg." Dee insisted that we wait for Dr. Kubiac. By the grace of God, Dr. Willis Kubiac, the legendary orthopedist, pieced my son's leg together the best that he could later that night.

When my son roused following surgery, he suffered terrible pain and a high fever caused by a raging infection. Dr. Kubiac purposefully left an egg-sized drainage hole in my son's calf, a wound that he feared might not heal. To make matters worse, my son was allergic to penicillin. "We'll have to wait and see," said Dr. Kubiac.

My boy had always been the one to cheer us with his smile that wouldn't quit. This time his smile quit. In his hospital room on the fourth floor of Riverside Hospital, my son turned his face to the wall and wouldn't turn back. He figured that his days as an athlete were over; we feared for his life. I had sent him on that fateful errand, breaking my promise to my wife. That Saturday was the darkest I'd ever known.

I braced myself the next morning to face the boy facing the wall. To my utter amazement, flying paper airplanes filled the air and covered the floor.

He paused from his folding long enough to say, "Dad, when they brought my body to the hospital, I wasn't there with it. I wouldn't accept what had happened to me. Last night, I counted and multiplied the tiles in the ceiling every conceivable way to keep my mind off what was. I refused to sleep or to see anyone. But, by late last night I knew I couldn't fight the truth any longer. I sighed and said, 'I don't have any more strength; I'm done for. I give up to You.' He heard me, Dad! You don't have to believe this, but as soon as I said that, alone in the middle of the night, I felt a quickening in my leg and warmth all over. For the first time since I came in here, I slept. When I woke up, Doc Kubiac stood at the foot of my bed saying to the nurse that the infection had turned. The hole was healing. I would keep my leg!"

The most recent thing my son said to me on this subject was, "Dad, I don't just pray to any God. I always pray to the very God who came to see me that Saturday night on the fourth floor of Riverside Hospital and saved my leg."

"Little Irrepressible" achieved grades during high school that earned him a place in an elite academic pre-med program. However, his staying in the program hung upon a final lab exam in Advanced Chemistry; he needed to earn an "A" in that exam and in that course. He assembled the complicated network of tubes and glassware called for by the experiment. At the last moment, he inadvertently struck the network with his arm, causing it to crash to the floor. Desperate, he ransacked the storeroom and found sufficient equipment, not yet cleaned up and dehumidified, to recreate the second attempt. Just then the teaching assistant announced, "You are too late getting started. Tear it down."

"Yes, Sir." As my son dismantled the equipment, he stopped and asked himself, "When have I ever gotten anywhere quitting like this?" He observed his classmates and noticed that none of the experiments were working. Realizing that he opposed the TA's orders and that he had a slim chance for success, he leaned against his desk and prayed, "O Lord, if you would ever like to give me a hand, this would be a good time." Then he resumed his experiment.

The TA had been working behind my son, hoping to have at least one successful experiment. When he turned around to find my son's experiment beautifully underway, he was elated. None of the experiments in any of the sections under the other TA's were working. Before he left the room for a few minutes, the TA said to my son, "I'll stay with you through the dinner hour to finish the experiment."

A nearby unit suddenly burst into flames, threatening the entire classroom. While other students stood paralyzed, my son swiftly smothered the fire with the only available extinguisher. He not only received an "A" for the course, his TA, who missed the fire show but became well aware of it afterwards, gave him the highest grade for "technique" because of his timely heroism.

After medical school, my son first worked in Alaska. When I recently saw the former junior high teacher who predicted his career behind bars, I guessed why she was eager to talk to me. She wanted to find out just how her prophecy had been fulfilled.

After trying to throw me off by inquiring about everyone else in the family, she finally asked, "And how is your son doing?"

Wishing to savor the conversation as long as I could, I replied, "He's working in Alaska." I knew that would sound as if he was exiled to an off-shore oil rig, which wouldn't surprise her.

She queried impatiently, "What's his position?"

"He works in a hospital."

I watched the wheels of her mind picturing him as an orderly or housekeeper. "I mean, what does he actually do?" she persisted.

"He's a physician."

There was an embarrassing pause. She said, "No, I mean the one I had in class!"

Only God Himself made it possible for me to respond solemnly, "Yes, that's who I mean."

While his mother took her last breath, about two months before I delivered this address, her son brought the farewell smile that I know lit her face by leading her, and the rest of us, in what had been our beloved bedtime prayer.

All praise to Thee, my God this night, for all the blessings of the light;
Keep me, O keep me, King of Kings, beneath the shadow of Thy wings.

My son taught me that God *will* find you anywhere, even on the fourth floor of a hospital, and even in the cereal aisle of a grocery store.

Figure 3: "Little Brother," by David M. Redding

My Father's Faith: Little Brother

My dad Charlie and his young brother, Blaine, were born to be "closer than a goose to its feathers." They lived under the benevolent regime of much older sisters and a remarkable mother whose time was pretty much consumed by their revered father. Their father, my grandfather, had returned from the War Between the States with a hacking cough, a consequence of all those nights sleeping on the cold ground. Although he managed to hew timber so fastidiously that not an axe mark appeared on the wood, my grandfather required much assistance to run their small farm on a remote ridge in West Virginia.

The domestic situation threw Charlie and Blaine together even more closely. When it came time to send Charlie off to first grade, Grandma admonished him, "Little Brother will have to go with you. Look after him; he's only four."

"Don't worry, Mom, I will."

In the frontier days of the late 1800s before the time of police and juries, every family aimed to develop a "scrapper" to beat off the bullies. Blaine became good at starting fights and turning them over to Charlie who became expert at ending them. It took their mutual adoration for these Siamese twins to survive.

Everybody had to work hard in those days; however, when Blaine "found" baseball, he would rather play than eat. While he was not Yogi Berra, the loquacious Yankee catcher, Blaine did resemble him. Like Yogi, he and Dad "graduated" from formal education in Charlie's fourth grade level to become athletic wonders in their neck of the woods. Even communities deep in the woods loved baseball, the only game there was in America.

Charlie became the crowd's captain and "Pretty Boy" Blaine became the darling of the fans. Blaine made left field the center of attention by his gift for making a difficult catch look impossible; he was often carried off the diamond when he made it the winning play. Charlie didn't mind; playing baseball was part of looking after

Little Brother. Besides, everyone knew Blaine made the catch as much for Charlie as for the team.

My father's favorite player was Honus Wagner, a gifted shortstop of the Pittsburgh Pirates. His statue stands today at the entrance of the Pittsburgh ballpark. The cost of his baseball card is the most exorbitant of any in either League. The Pittsburgh Pirates eventually offered the two brothers, Blaine and Charlie, contracts.

One Sunday afternoon, before the brothers were to have left home to join the Pirates, Charlie was pitching a winning game. While watching for the catcher's signal, he noticed his dad's grey beard hanging over the backstop, and a finger beckoning under it. He approached respectfully, prepared to hear about breaking the Sabbath day. "Sonny, I thought I taught you better than this," the old Civil War veteran said and then left the diamond. Charlie walked slowly back to the mound; limp with remorse, he lost the game.

Just at this watershed in the lives of the brothers, Pine Grove Church, a tiny church up the hill above their farm on Yellow Creek, pitched a revival tent. The Reddings had not been churchgoers, however, the indulgent sisters had grown concerned about their brothers' associations with loose girls. At supper one night, Sarah, whom everyone called "Sad," proposed that the family attend the final night of revival. She and her sisters counted on their wild brothers being converted. Jesus, they figured, would never be nearer to them than at the foot of that sawdust trail.

Reluctantly the brothers agreed. Charlie warned his family not to take any promises he made too seriously during the excitement of the service; he knew he would likely break them as soon as he arrived home. Nonetheless, the family filled a row of benches expectantly. As the revival took hold, both brothers not only walked down the aisle for conversion, they also accepted the call to preach the gospel. To everyone's utter amazement, they next declined the fantastic contracts offered them by the Pirates.

Instead they made plans to attend Cleveland Bible School. The school required six months to secure them the diplomas they needed, partly to compensate for their smattering of elementary education. They also had personal matters to make straight.

One day Charlie was in the stable watching Blaine saddle up to visit a family they admired, who lived up the valley. He was always being asked to sing, a talent that Charlie was denied. On the harness rack hung an expensive silver-ornamented leather strap that Charlie had never noticed before. "Blaine, where did that come from?"

Blaine replied, "Now that we've been converted, I've got to confess. I took it from the stable of the family that I'm on my way to visit today."

Horrified, Charlie tossed the strap over Little Brother's saddle, still carrying out his mother's assignment to look after him. "You can't wait any longer to return it!"

"Charlie, I could drown myself or jump from the cliff that I'll pass this morning; but, there's no way on earth that I could admit to those wonderful friends who think the world of us that I'm a thief." He tossed the silver strap back to his brother and mounted his horse.

Charlie caught the strap and tossed it right back to Blaine. "Don't come back until you settle this with them. Otherwise our conversion was just a publicity stunt reflecting against our whole family including you."

As Blaine rode off he called, "I'll take it, but I won't take it back."

The day turned into an incredibly long one. As the shadow of evening stretched heavy across the farm and Little Brother still had not come home, Charlie grew apprehensive. In recent months, Blaine had come down with something like the flu that he couldn't quite shake off. As the first star appeared, Charlie walked into the yard thinking that Blaine's ailment might be responsible for the delay. He noticed too that the sisters watched and listened intently by the open window.

The Reddings lived near bluffs and promontories that broke up the valley. In certain locations a shout could create multiple echoes. Finally, in the distance, the family heard Blaine singing the Hallelujah Chorus. Until the day he died, Dad insisted that he counted seven after echoes. When Blaine finally rode dead-tired into the farm, he said, "Charlie, I took it back."

That Revival, along with its consequences of cancelled baseball contracts and Blaine's return of stolen tack, were big events in that rural community. The community also treasured Blaine's singing and praying. In the days before movies and television, Blaine was not only the life of any gathering, he also was called upon to sing and offer up one of his heart-rending prayers. Dad said, "No one I ever heard before or since, could pray the heart out of heaven like my Little Brother. And that night before we left for Bible School, I could hear my brother's touch of vanity gradually vanish from his presentation."

Blaine's illness eventually proved fatal. It was an unspeakable, incurable curse that became the major tragedy in my father's life. No one ever spoke the shameful name of the disease, but everyone knew what was killing the young man they loved dearly. It progressed rapidly into paresis – the softening of the brain – that eventually drove Blaine stark raving mad. My father never blamed his brother; he blamed himself. He had promised his mother to look after Little Brother.

He believed he had failed utterly, and never forgave himself for losing Blaine to that insatiable curse.

The brothers managed to graduate from the Cleveland Bible School. Soon afterwards, the family and close friends gathered for the unavoidable last evening at Yellow Creek before Charlie took Little Brother to the Cleveland Hospital for the Insane. That last evening, Dad later said, seemed taken over by God Himself. Everyone expected that Blaine would "bear witness" to his powerful spiritual experience, but no one anticipated his tears or the words to the old gospel melody that became his confession. At first, Blaine sang in whispers, tentatively, then firmly, bringing all the people gathered to their feet:

> *O be careful what you sow*
> *For your seed will surely grow;*
> *And he who sows his seed today*
> *Shall reap tomorrow*
> *With joy or sorrow.*

Although the actions that led to the contraction of his fatal disease still shocked the community, his family and friends insisted that Blaine deliver the benediction that night that should have marked the beginning of his ministry. He was still their darling.

The trip to the hospital took many days on horseback, Dad told me. Charlie couldn't risk the train, nor could he afford an ambulance. He would personally look after Little Brother who was such a big part of himself.

The last visit that Charlie made to see his brother took almost a week by horseback. The 1900s were still new and it was years before World War I. Miraculously, he found Blaine to be completely himself. It was like old times. They were back together again like always. And, no spells marred that sacred farewell. As the fateful day drew to its close, Blaine said to his brother, "Charlie, I love you better than I ever loved anybody in all the world. I kept just one secret from you, but now I can't remember what it was."

Charlie laid Little Brother to rest outside the window of Pine Grove Church where they took the vows together. The little church still stands. Charlie had remained faithful to his mother's words, "Take care of your Little Brother," from the day he left home for first grade until the end.

Figure 4: "The U.S.S. Saratoga: 27° List," by David M. Redding

IN HARM'S WAY: MY WORLD WAR II

My children's godmother, a very proper Presbyterian, relaxed late one evening sufficiently to share this true story with Dee and me, providing I would promise never to use it in the pulpit. As soon as she told the story I knew that I could never keep that promise. A first grader was trying on sweaters at a department store. Suddenly the little fellow exclaimed, "This isn't a V-neck sweater, is it?" "Why do you care about that?" his mother queried. "My teacher was wearing a V-neck sweater when she leaned over my desk to check my paper and one of her lungs fell out!" Frightening things frequently happened to our family that turned out to be not only bearable, but laughable.

In Harm's Way had been a way of life at home for me. The Depression meant the church could not pay my preaching father, so I spent my boyhood on a remote wilderness farm while another kind of depression hospitalized my beloved father. Mother's touch at the piano eased my anxious little sister and me to sleep at night. I still remember the reassurance of "There Is a Balm in Gilead." Eventually, God brought my beloved father home, which made it easy for me to believe: Jesus would return for us all.

Dad's "blues," as Lincoln called his depressions, were hard enough to bear, but one night after my sister and I had gone to bed, Dad solemnly closed the kitchen door, which he never did, and it riveted my sister and me to the floor where enough light and sound came through for us to overhear.

The domestic atmosphere had grown heavy but we could not believe what Dad said. "Mother, I'm afraid I'm going to hurt somebody, maybe myself." We hardly had strength to scramble back to bed, when they blew out the kerosene lamp. No one in our undeveloped Ohio wilderness had electricity or phones.

The next day with his arm around me, Dad assigned me to look after Mom and my little sister, to milk our two cows and gather the eggs. I had no dearer friend than my father, only a mighty Percheron, a collie, and no neighbors. We walked a mile to the old school's bus when it was running. "Hang on," he said, "I'll be back." When my dad was gone it was it seemed "forever." But I knew he'd keep his word, if he didn't die, sick as he was. I told God I'd never make it if anything happened to him. I asked my mother every night if Dad was coming back. She nodded the tears away, and with her piano we could sleep.

Mr. Jordan came by with groceries in his 1929 Chevy panel truck, when it wasn't too muddy. Mom traded him eggs and butter I churned for what she needed. Curious neighbors came by. One boy hissed to his mother, "Is his dad really crazy?" Late summer, I stumbled across a flourishing wild huckleberry patch. It made a great trade with Mr. Jordan.

Finally, after "forever" was overdoing it, we got a letter Dad was coming home. His sisters were picking him up. I kept the letter under my pillow.

The biggest day of my life began long before the sun got up. When it did I went out to swing on the front gate. Mom packed a lunch but I couldn't eat. About 1:30, which was almost after "forever," I heard a car in the distance. I leaped from the gate and literally flew over the hill. God wouldn't fool me.

The car stopped, a big guy got out, knelt down, and folded me in his arms. "Promise me, Dad, you'll never go again." "I won't." And he never did. After that I had no trouble believing that Jesus was coming back. My Dad did. I could believe anything then, but it was awhile before I let him out of my sight, and he let me sleep at the foot of his bed. I left him later. But he never left me.

When I was a teenager, World War II took hold and patriotism inflamed our nation. Like so many teenagers in the 1940s, I longed to wear a sailor's uniform and become a parading hero featured on the front page of the local newspapers. Before I knew it, it was my turn to put to sea.

The night before I flew to the naval base in San Francisco, I asked Dad to pray for me. He said he would if I sang his favorite song of mine; it was the only time I ever remember his voice breaking. My mother accompanied me on the piano as I sang the words of the Psalm she taught me the year Dad was gone. It got me through World War II:

Lead me, Lord,
Lead me in Thy righteousness,
Make Thy way plain
Before my face;

> *For it is Thou, O Lord,*
> *Thou, O Lord, only*
> *That makest me dwell*
> *In safety. (From Psalms 5:8 and 4:8)*

Being in the Navy meant daily showers. Until then, I had bathed once a week, using the same water in the washtub that my sister had used on Saturday night. Being in the Navy also meant that beautiful girls thronged us at every terminal station or airport with sandwiches and inviting smiles. "You'll soon forget your old girlfriends," we were told, even though we'd been spoken for. I knew I would never leave mine. Out at sea one time, we didn't receive mail for three months. At the next mail call, I received seventy-five letters from a girl who signed off with her initials "M.M.M." I stacked them up on my desk and began reading. Halfway through the stack, I realized that the girl I really loved most was Dee, and broke off with beautiful "M.M.M."

What harm could come to me on that beautiful tropical blue sea? I felt as though by day I could fly like the fish escaping their submarine predator, and, by night, find my way by the light of the phosphorescence that lit the Pacific. And, of course there was always the sacred gold braid that charmed my sleeve through two voyages around the world aboard ships like the Battleship Idaho and amusing tours of duty like L.S.T. 122.

My first home at sea was a converted merchant marine ship. The best she could do was twelve knots, which meant a three-month journey to the South Pacific conflict. At night the only light allowed was the phosphorescence glowing in the water. A lit cigarette or flashlight could lead to a court martial.

One night when we were anchored in port we requested permission to come aboard wearing white gloves, as the Officer's Manual directed. It amused the Deck Officer who could tell we hadn't worn our dress outfit since we left Midshipman School at Columbia. A gruff permission from the Captain's Cabin greeted our, "Reporting for duty, Sir." He was barebacked and drunk, able only to point at his crème de menthe bottle, and then fall over. His name was Champagne, and he was commissioned by an Admiral whose skin he'd saved by steering the flagship to port instead of to starboard as the Admiral had mistakenly ordered.

Captain Champagne was not as bad as his introduction suggests, but he was so full of braggadocio that all of us young officers participated in sending for the rickshaw driver who had been hawking our ship with "Beautiful fresh Russian girl I bring you." They brought her up the gangway, the hairiest specimen you ever saw, and shoved her in the Cap'n's cabin while we gathered at the porthole.

The Captain was equal to the challenge. He pointed to his trophy Japanese sword hanging by his bunk and growled, "First thing we'll have to do is shave those legs." Seeing that gesture, our Siberian beauty scrambled to the port and flew down the gangway, maybe to a convent.

During our journey toward the South Pacific, America dropped the bombs on Hiroshima and Nagasaki, stopping the war. Our ship was practically in the wake of the U.S.S Indianapolis; the Indianapolis delivered the two nuclear warheads to the Enola Gay. In a tragic irony, two Japanese torpedoes sank the U.S.S. Indianapolis soon afterwards, taking 1500 sailors to their deaths. It was the worst disaster in our Naval history, and it felt close to home. While it's "cool" now to condemn the use of our nuclear bombs, we knew first hand that the Japanese were ready to commit hari-kari to save their honor. Battlements and pillboxes covered Japanese beaches; it would have taken up to a million more American boys to stop the aggression. As terrible as the nuclear bombs were, I'm convinced that they saved a million of us American youngsters.

In some ways, World War II lasted forever. You would think so too, if you had crossed the Pacific twice at ten to twelve knots as we did, looking for the battleship, the U.S.S. Idaho. Along the way, we did man the machine guns for pirates and communists, in the last days of Chiang Kai-shek, as we hauled our cargo of flour up the Yangtze River in China, past the city known then as Nanking (now Nanjing) to the starving people of Hankow (now Hankou).

In other ways, the war happened overnight. We eventually faced the most destructive enemy of all; who would have guessed it: the weather. At twenty-one years of age and following nearly four years of active service, I had become a Deck Officer. We had transferred to the U.S.S. Saratoga, our legendary aircraft carrier, which was loaded with thousands of semi-seasoned veterans. We were heading home on the beautiful blue sea and passing through the tropics. Where's the harm in that? It turned out that we were on a collision course with a typhoon that endangered our entire homeward bound fleet and became eligible for the worst storm of the century. At first we laughed it off because of the Sara's size. But, as the winds increased their fury, all hands were ordered below, all watertight ports were clamped tight, and waves surpassing one hundred feet tossed us like debris. We stopped laughing. The memory of the burial at sea of men we knew on the U.S.S. Indianapolis was too raw, and we felt the jaws of death gaping before us.

Our decks pitched bow down and stern up while, at the same time, the ship rolled like a pendulum from port to starboard. We were afraid we were going to die, then we were afraid that we wouldn't. We became a city of doomed sailors. The sight or smell of food brought up whatever was left inside of us. The Saratoga became a hospital for a thousand seasick sailors. Sickbay took over the passageways, lined with cots of the retching. Those of us who managed to eat at the urging of our old petty officer had potatoes and beans sliding into our laps when the ship entered its roll. At a certain place in the roll, all the lights went out. We heard loose marbles bouncing, as well as chairs and tables scraping the decks above and below us. Then, when we reached the limit of our roll, we heard, closer than we would like, some mate throwing up.

The cook finally gave up his battle with the tumbling pots and pans; he announced on the loudspeaker, perhaps as the cook did on the sinking Edmund Fitzgerald, "Fellows, it's too rough to feed ya." Our table was the only one that had any stragglers left.

The main expression of a ship's distress during a storm is how close it comes during a roll to reaching the "critical list." That is when the roll turns her over, entombing everyone on board. We rolled to port to the point of the critical list; if memory serves me right, ours was 27 degrees. The ship shuddered, seemingly paralyzed. Each one of us wondered, is this it? Later my sister told me that she overheard Mother sobbing prayers for me all night. Was it then? Somehow the Saratoga righted herself and rolled to the critical list on her starboard side. Shuddered. After an eternity, she rolled back.

That experience welded all our ship's company together forever. You know what love is? It's the bond that's forged with those who share the same sinking ship with you. Afterwards we discovered that many ships sank during that typhoon; it had presented the most terrible battle. For some reason, God spared the old Saratoga. A newer ship now bears her name but there will never be another like the original for those of us who prayed through harm's way to end our World War II experience with an act of God.

Singer and songwriter Gordon Lightfoot caught the ordeal in his ballad, "The Wreck of the Edmund Fitzgerald":

> *The legend lives on from the Chippewa on down*
> *Of the big lake they call Gitche Gumee*

The lake, it is said, never gives up her dead
When the skies of November turn gloomy . . .
The dawn came late and the breakfast had to wait
When the gales of November came slashing
When afternoon came it was freezing rain
In the face of a hurricane West Wind . . .

When suppertime came the old cook came on deck
Saying, "Fellows, it's too rough to feed ya."
At seven PM a main hatchway caved in
He said, "Fellas, it's been good to know ya."

The impact of this experience resonated through my life in unexpected ways. Some years later during the 1960s I was called to the pulpit of Flagler Presbyterian Church in St. Augustine, Florida. It remains one of two historic buildings of America's oldest city (the other being the old fort), and attracts more tourists than any other church in the United States. Many ministers with enviable credentials had applied to or prayed to become its minister. At that time I was without a church, and had a conspirator on site, who lived on Aviles Street operating what she called "The Knitting Basket." She was my beloved Aunt Alice and Godmother. Formerly a nurse at Presbyterian Hospital in New York City, Aunt Alice had saved my life as an infant, endearing her to my mother who had lost three previous infants without her. We also shared the same birthday.

Well, Aunt Alice undertook my pulpit campaign with the same ability and devotion that she had given to nursing. She had the huge advantage over my adversaries of being known and loved as a fellow church member of the pulpit committee. She also understood that Southern churches would naturally regard any Yankee candidate such as myself with some misgivings. She gave the skeptical committee the scrapbook she had religiously kept all the life of her beloved godson. This scrapbook, along with my academic credentials and generous references, was enough for that twenty-four member Pastoral Search Committee to offer me the position of minister.

One problem challenged me from the beginning of negotiations: the manse, which was almost sacred, for Flagler built that too. It was a tourist attraction – a fishbowl for all the tourist busses and carriages – and a woman killer encompassing three massive floors. Orthopedic physicians had determined that Dee could lead a cautious normal life, for a minister's wife, if her homestead occupied only one floor. She must avoid stairs. So, the Pulpit Committee prayerfully promised me that they would see to it that we could buy or rent our own house.

Upon arrival at St. Augustine, we were shocked to discover that the Pulpit Committee had not told the Trustees of their promise to us. When the Trustees learned that we did not intend to live in the manse, they became furious and hostile. Tradition dictated that even as all Flagler ministers in the past had lived in the manse, all future ministers would as well.

Dick Cozad, a trustee who was also an active leader of Session, led the unalterable position of the Trustees. They would be flexible on other issues but not this one. This gem of a church, which by that time seemed like one we couldn't live without, was slipping from our hands. In our temporary quarters, Dee and I faced this crisis together. We prayed.

I took the most recalcitrant trustee to lunch. We circled the table for the strategic seat, finally sat down, and stared at our menus. We ordered. Dick asked me if I had served in the War, a topic that was still contemporary. I replied, "Yes." He assumed as a chaplain? "No."

"What arm of the service?"

"Navy."

"What did you do?"

"I was a deck officer in the South Pacific."

Dick pushed back his chair and stood up. Then he said, "Were you ever in harm's way?"

"Yes, coming home in the big typhoon."

"What ship were you on?"

"The Saratoga."

Immediately Dick was by my side. He put his arms around me and wept. "I was on it with you when we nearly went down." I thought he was not going to release me.

Later, at the combined meeting of the Session and Trustees, we still had to settle this issue of our housing. I wondered what Dick would do; he was the first to speak. "I've thought about this, and we've got to do whatever Dave wants. I move he be granted permission to rent or buy a house." There was no further discussion; it was seconded and passed.

My shipmate Commander Dick Cozad died two years later. The man he worked with told me that he referred to me after that as his best friend. To Dee and me, he was an act of God.

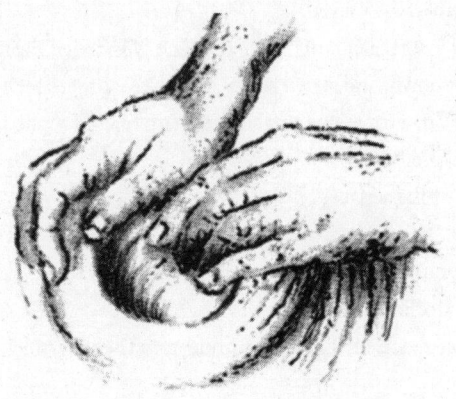

Figure 5: "The Hey Day of Laity Creativity," by David M. Redding

The Source of the River Is Sacred

> Oh, the joys of those who do not follow the advice of the wicked, or stand around with sinners, or join in with mockers.
> But they delight in the law of the Lord, meditating on it day and night.
> They are like trees planted along the riverbank, bearing fruit each season.
> Their leaves never wither, and they prosper in all they do. But not the wicked!
> They are like worthless chaff, scattered by the wind.
> They will be condemned at the time of judgment.
> Sinners will have no place among the godly.
> For the Lord watches over the path of the godly,
> but the path of the wicked leads to destruction.[2]

Jack Benny's funniest line on radio was when he was "stuck up," and said nothing when the robber demanded, "Your money or your life." When prodded, he explained, "I'm thinking. I'm thinking."

Bill Cody, the Laity Lodge Director, had put out a papal edict, "No pets." But he was also excited about scheduling Dr. Louis Hadley Evans of the gigantic Bel Air Presbyterian Church, and later National Presbyterian Church, that he let him bring his dog. His retriever was as big as a horse, and he romped all over us. I think my funniest line here at Laity was, "Next year I'm going to bring my dog." That proposition brought down the house.

My almost forty years as guest speaker here ends today. Emily Dickinson wrote:

---

[2] New Living Translation (NLT), Holy Bible, copyright © 1996, 2004 by Tyndale Charitable Trust. Used by permission of Tyndale House Publishers. Psalm 1.

*The capacity to terminate
is a specific grace.*

Four of my eight children have had to come here today to make up for my incapacity. What I lacked in depth, I made up in length. I came here for two weekends for many years, as well as two weeks annually, and a time or two, four weeks, due to others' cancellations (a grace I denied you). However, you must surely recognize by now that I could not bear to sacrifice so treasured an audience lightly. My beloved Dee's abrupt departure may have been her way of saying, "You've had enough."

Fearing that my perpetual tenure was hard for you to bear, it has comforted me to have several insist that the major obstacle to Laity Lodge is the two and one half hour expedition from the San Antonio airport bussed like sardines, in a vehicle so swollen with suitcases in the back that now and then one broke loose to bounce upon someone's head still tender from last year.

But you know, that trip which could be arduous for arthritic bones became a memorable pilgrimage for me due to Eddie Sears, the former Laity Lodge Associate Director.

Of course we love scholarly Howard Hovde, Laity Lodge Director for many years, for rupturing himself daily with hefty armloads of spellbinding study books, and for his Carole for rescuing us with finer fare from diabetic comas caused by feasts of potatoes and gravy that Eulalia fattened us with. Those of us not quite reformed could still look forward to Jim Morris's fudge, late Thursday nights. And if you stayed in Black Bluff you could hope to be invited to the party where the twine hung out swinging by your deck on its way to the mouth-watering vintages, cooling in the Frio.

But Eddie Sears, who called himself Mr. Goodwrench, redeemed my commute from the airport. For years he never failed to pick me up, always right on time. By the time we had passed the town of Comfort, he had given me the indispensible funny story I had to have to maintain my reputation. Eddie generously let me take credit for the story. We laughed the trip away, because he always reassured me my dinner would be kept warm, reacquainting me with the flora and fauna of our tiny Eden here at the Source of the River, as sacred to us as to the Celts.

Eddie is one of those transplanted hybrid Texans. When Bird Osborne died, he shared Bird's beautiful city with me; one might say that he gave me her Corpus Christi. He shared the secret of his General Store in Hunt, "If we don't have it, you don't need it." And when he feared his supermarket might threaten

H.E.B. he sold it. He made sure I saw Fredericksburg as the memorial to the World War II's Admiral Nimitz.

As Eddie showed me, even the roads to Laity Lodge were hospitable, unless you turn left when you leave the gate. My daughter Marion and I were commuting daily to San Antonio when Dee was first hospitalized for her heart, was it eight or nine years ago? Trusting Texas Highway courtesy signs blurred by . . . signs that "suggested" fines were doubled if you exceeded forty miles per hour in the construction zone. Our Diz was sick, so we stuck to seventy until blinking lights ruined our rear view.

"S'matter, can't you read the sign?"

"What do you mean? Since it was after hours and no one was working, and I could see no traffic all the way to El Paso, I disregarded it just as I paid no attention to the sign that said 'Watch for ice on the bridge' since it was midsummer, or just as I ignored the sign that said, 'Slow, high water' since it's been bone dry."

He looked grim as he marched back to his car . . . I feared to write me up, but instead he drove off in a shower of gravel.

I figured he was Eddie Sears in a trooper's uniform.

Thanks to Howard Butt's global vision, the harvest of Laity Lodge is not facts but friendship including some of Christianity's renowned. England's grand old wizard of laughter, Editor of the prestigious *Punch*, Malcolm Muggeridge, introduced the world to Mother Teresa, through his video and volume, *Something Beautiful for God*. She converted him as well as how many more of us. He narrowly escaped his most traumatic moment when his canoe capsized in the Frio.

By far my favorite psychotherapist was the Swiss author, Dr. Paul Tournier. He graced this place with his most remarkable experience. It was about his birth as an author.

After Tournier had written his first manuscript, his publisher had suggested he find a friend to proof it. He selected his Greek professor, though he was an atheist, and Tournier's book was Christian. The old professor agreed to do it, but explained his eyes were weak and asked Paul to read him the first chapter. Paul did, waiting for the fireworks from the bitter unbeliever. But his old teacher responded, "Paul, continuez."

Paul read the second chapter and to Tournier's mounting surprise, his beloved skeptic repeated the same refrain, "Paul, continuez." Tournier read to him the third chapter, after which his professor said, "Paul, we must pray together."

After prayer Paul could not wait to say, "Professor, I didn't know you were a Christian."

"Oh, yes."

"When did you become a Christian?"

With tears in his eyes, the old don replied, "Just now."

One of our most exciting visitors stayed two weeks. Alexander Ginsburg was a refugee with political asylum from the Soviet Union. During the Cold War he was a close friend of author Alexander Solzhenitsyn, who had entrusted him with his royalties to be given to the persecuted families of Christian and Jewish prisoners. He soon became one of those prisoners of the Gulag himself.

Liberty Church had become fascinated with the cry "Free Ginsburg," which often happened when the letter-writing campaign made the prisoner's file become alarmingly fat from the global outcry.

Dee had discovered the prayer of Solzhenitsyn in *Vogue* magazine. The prayer had entered this country through *Samizdat,* the underground, remarkable to me for the astounding sentence, "You created a path for me through despair." It was the first we heard of Solzhenitsyn in the West. Alexander Solzhenitsyn thankfully gave me the copyright rights to that prayer.

Liberty Church was soon involved in filling Ginsburg's file with letters pleading for the freedom of another innocent victim. It worked, for Ginsburg came to this country, first visiting Liberty Church to thank us. He was convinced that we had freed him from the Gulag's grip. Working with the media, we helped launch his national speaking schedule. Ohio State University paid an honorarium of $3,500.00 for him to speak, as did every other location all over the country where he spoke. The largest proportion of the funds went to the families of Gulag prisoners. But he spoke first to Liberty Church, refusing any payment from us.

He not only became a famous former prisoner and journalist, he also was charismatic, the life of the party. He stayed with us a few days, still struggling with his English. Dee had worked hours to get the Russian black bread to come out right for him. However, he passed it up declaring, "That's all I ever got in Lubyanka, and the Gulag."

We learned that he was the unique convict, brave enough to stand up to the warden. When we asked what was hardest for him, he said, "The screams of the others." In one of our small groups here on the Frio we went around the circle with the question, "What is your particular gift?" He answered, "I believe my gift is to be a prisoner." That made me forget my gift. My boys, seeing him limp down the hallway, could see what the beatings had done to him. My pain in the neck seemed trifling beside the torture this little man had taken on behalf of these millions of forgotten martyrs.

Natalya Solzhenitsyn told me that they had come to expect one imprisonment to addict a victim to vodka. Ginsburg had had three imprisonments, and of course I profited from his misery. I had told him early on about Alcoholics Anonymous, and have permission to share that I introduced him to Don Legge, a leading figure in A.A. Ginsburg sat in a window in Black Bluff, resistant with arms crossed, as he must have faced many a grilling from a warden. But not long after he departed, I received a phone call from Paris. My secretary announced it from an open upstairs window, fortunately within hearing of a meeting of ministers in our churchyard. I took the call upstairs. It was Ginsburg who said he needed the phone number of that AA member friend of mine. It was my last communication with him

I must share Ginsburg's triumphant Creativity Week. He worked quietly a week on a project in copper. I had feared all along for his censure that I felt would be forthcoming for our preoccupation here with tennis, to him, I am sure, a rich man's game. When he finished his copper project, he carried it down to our courts. The forbidding concentration camp fence stopped him momentarily; then he came inside. He spotted Henry Parish (the Laity Lodge tennis instructor), his favorite, and presented him with his handiwork, a copper tennis ball.

A big night we will remember at Laity Lodge was presented by God's creativity. It was the night of David Tolley's (composer/pianist) concert. By late afternoon it was growing dark. An ominous storm was gathering strength. Its thunder and lightning made us forget past storms. It shook the Great Hall. In the middle of his concert, the lights went out. David's crescendo joined the cosmic accompaniment. He was performing "The Phantom of the Opera." He never stopped playing, though he didn't even have a flashlight to read his music. No one left. They couldn't see, and were paralyzed less by terror than by exaltation.

Coinciding with his finale, the lights came on as if prearranged, and our august Founder in his coat and tie, stood up on the new sofa, still in his shoes, and in a sonorous voice proclaimed that night to be the most awesome Laity Lodge had ever had.

It is hard to close with close friends here, that God has hand selected. We have eaten three meals daily together and sat beside each other for six days. The easiest access to distinguished physicians vastly strengthened the Texas connection to my life. I have to mention Dr. Lane Bicknell, my lifelong friend, who surgically saved my life before he said goodbye, passing on his reverent affection for David, the Shepherd Boy in his Creative Writing piece two years ago. And last year, when Dee's foot was breaking out in the wounds that eventually wore down her life, Dr. George Smith, my dear friend, treated her as tenderly as his own mother. And my good friend, Dr. David Hughes, is here this year. If I had time I would say something about each of you here, but Louis Ridgeway helped me with my wounds, and Edith Frick, like so many of you, helped John build our church barn. Ora Lee Seale's dozen flowering pear trees were in magnificent bloom during the services for Dee. Our dear Sally McCollum represented you all superbly at the services, and pitched in like a sister to Marion and Sandy, back at the house afterwards. I could go on....

There's no end to my indebtedness to this place, down to my tennis friends and enemies who never missed in almost forty years, like Henry Parrish, Al Brann, Beth Hughes and Jimmy Thomas, to say nothing of every single one of you who came today – to make sure I'm out of here at last.

Our spiritual father, founder and example, Howard, continues to counsel me on the radio in Ohio, 8:30 in the mornings. He and Barbara Dan not only blazed my trail, but in the dark they shined their headlights for me.

They gave Dee and me a big long weekend in San Antonio when Dee had her first heart crisis . . . and her Tim Duncan, the Admiral, and the Spurs provided great entertainment in the basketball tournament. Then a few years ago when she was still able to enjoy the Riverwalk, we were both "pumped" about going again. And this last Father's Day weekend, Marion and I were able to take full advantage of the luxury we had planned for Dee to recover from the strain of travel before this grand finale week.

Almost ten years ago, Dee and I were on our way into San Antonio between retreats, and were about ready to whiz past Kerrville, but Dee said softly, as she said everything (except when I had yanked on the unthinkable tie) "David, we've got to get to an Emergency room, now. It's my heart."

Stricken, I knew exactly where to go. They told us, "You would never have made it to San Antonio in time." We made it later by ambulance, with Kerrville's crucial support, and we were quickly ensconced in a crowded patient ward built for soldiers who fought for Stonewall Jackson.

Our first and only visitors were Howard and Barbara Dan. That meant more than I can say. Soon after they left, and don't think we didn't put two and two together, Dee was moved to the new wing, rivaling the refurbished Presbyterian Hospital in New York. Dee was saved for her final game, along with the Spurs' victory.

Wasn't that an earthly rehearsal of the unfolding heavenly plan for his faithful and beloved servant He gave me for almost sixty years? Her last mortal goal was to be with you here today. By March she knew it was not to be. She reminds me today to thank Howard and Barbara Dan who included her in my visits here, and brought her such friendship, and the joyful kinship of this canyon.

Help me, God, to remember how she taught me how to dance.

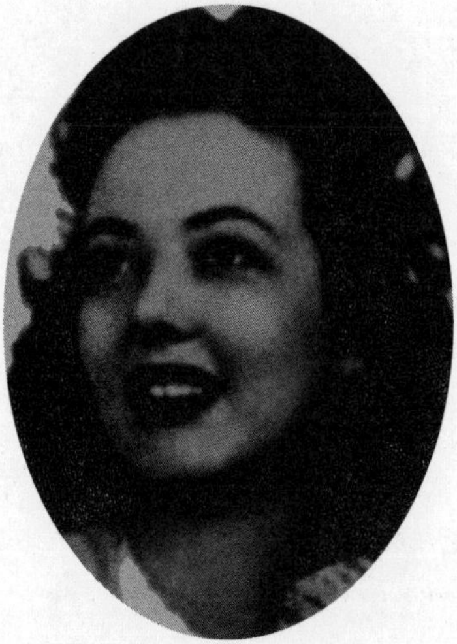

You Taught Me How to Dance

BY DAVID A. REDDING
(WITH APOLOGIES TO "MISS POTTER")

It's a painful triumph for
My Dee to get here Sundays, anymore,
Tied to a chair and perched on wheels;
Why, she used to teach the Marines how to swim,
And I had a showpiece jitterbug
To teach me how to dance.
You caught me, Dear, with your sky blue eyes;
And with your beguiling arms around me,
You made a sailor brainless.
So, I'm still ready to dance with you forever.
How time flies! It only seems like yesterday.

This also applies to the nearly forty years all of you took
To show me how to let down my hair and
Dance on the banks of the Frio.
But I won't forget that night
My partner got the steps across to me, till all of you,
And I know it must have seemed forever—
Finally encircled a wooden legged preacher
Who only said he loved you till
You taught him how to dance
In here.[4]

---

[4] For Liberty, and Laity, October 14, 2007.

TABLE OF FIGURES

FIGURE 1: "FIVE SMOOTH STONES: THE SHEPHERD BOY," BY DAVID M. REDDING — viii

FIGURE 2: "THE ACCIDENT," BY DAVID M. REDDING — 6

FIGURE 3: "LITTLE BROTHER," BY DAVID M. REDDING — 12

FIGURE 4: "THE U.S.S. SARATOGA: 27° LIST," BY DAVID M. REDDING — 18

FIGURE 5: "THE HEY DAY OF LAITY CREATIVITY," BY DAVID M. REDDING — 26

A Word about the Artist: David M. Redding

The five pencil drawings are by the author's son, David M. Redding. His wildlife paintings have been on exhibit in the historic buildings of the Princeton University and many other galleries. Several major exhibits include those at the Cleveland Metroparks Zoo, the Columbus Zoo, and Houston's Museum of the West.

David is also one of the two key ministers of the largest Presbyterian Church in the Midwest, Central College Church in greater Columbus, Ohio. David and his wife, Bobbie, were at Laity Lodge last fall, when he spoke at the Singles' Retreat. They have a daughter, Alicia (who also has a daughter, Ava), and two sons, Ian and Cameron.

About the Author: David A. Redding

Editorials for *Life* magazine and a feature he wrote for *Reader's Digest* plunged author David A. Redding into publishing twenty-five books. *He Never Spoke without a Parable* is his life's work. Harper and Row did well with his earlier work, *The Parables He Told*, in the late 1970s, but this latest, comprehensive rendition is far more entertaining and enriched with recent scholarship. He released Volumes I, II, and III-V of this creation in 2000, 2001, and 2002.

Dr. Redding has been the minister of the renowned Flagler Memorial Presbyterian Church in St. Augustine, Florida, and the celebrated Liberty Presbyterian Church, the Amish built timber-frame cathedral in Delaware, Ohio. He is also treasured across the country as an inspiring speaker, and quoted in popular radio ministry programs and best-selling book collections of poignant stories. His preaching and writing are enhanced by his homespun, spellbinding, story telling ability. David is available for motivational conferences, spiritual retreats, and other speaking engagements on his website, www.davidredding.com.

David and his wife, Dorothy McCleery Redding, have eight children. Marion and David M. (Bobbie) are ministers. John (Shari) is a custom homebuilder who was the Construction Manager for Liberty's Barn Church. Mark (Sarah) is a pediatrician, and founder and Executive Director of the Community Health Access Project (C.H.A.P.). Rob (Pam) is a hotel executive, Chris (Pam) a restaurateur and Datil Do It Sauce inventor, Sandy (Fred) is an executive in health care and a wife, mother and grandmother extraordinaire, and Phúc is our Vietnamese businesswoman and cosmetic genius. The family still gathers in the old stone house they built together on a farm by the Scioto River famous for Tecumseh.

"Fifty years ago I thought I knew all about everything Christian. Today, I'm still trying to understand many things Jesus said – and I've been helped immeasurably by this new book from David A. Redding... It makes me feel as if I'm standing in the crowds listening to Jesus, and getting the message."

DONALD T. KAUFFMAN, AUTHOR AND EDITOR